Jessica Casey

and Other Works

by Away With Words

Edited by
MARY MADEC

DVD animation by visual artist
AIDEEN BARRY and the Away With Words Writers

salmonpoetry

The *Away With Words* project is supported by:

Published in 2012 by
Salmon Poetry
Cliffs of Moher, County Clare, Ireland
Website: www.salmonpoetry.com
Email: info@salmonpoetry.com

EDITED BY: *Mary Madec*
COVER IMAGE: *Aideen Barry*
COVER DESIGN: *Siobhán Hutson*

Salmon Poetry receives financial support from The Arts Council

i.m. Michael Diskin, Manager of the Townhall Theatre
who opened doors to those who support people with intellectual
disabilities participate in the arts in Galway

AWAY WITH WORDS is grateful for the support and encouragement we have received from many people which helped to bring this project to completion:

*Our colleagues and staff at
the Brothers of Charity services*

The Galway Arts Community

*Coláiste Iognáid transition year students
Síofra Leonard and Aifric Henry Bruen*

*The Davoren Family, Corcullen,
and their beautiful Connemara pony, Tír na nÓg*

The Carphone Warehouse

Boots, Galway

Mez's Masquarade, Galway

Aer Arann Islands

The G Hotel

Contents

SINGLE POEMS

Section 1 – Inclusion Ireland Winners

Section 2 – People Who Inspire

Section 3 – Ordinary Life

INTRODUCTION

Jessica Casey and Other Works is the first formal publication of AWAY WITH WORDS, an innovative arts project to explore creativity through writing. It was dreamed up in 2008 by Claude and Mary Madec and set up as a collaboration between local writers and That's Life (an initiative of the Brothers of Charity Services in County Galway to support people with intellectual disabilities to engage in the arts life of their communities). This publication marks the fifth anniversary of AWAY WITH WORDS, and we are delighted that The Arts Council, Salmon Poetry and Cúirt are associated with this event.

AWAY WITH WORDS offers a variety of writing workshops and writing retreats where participants get a chance to explore their imaginations and discover their voices under the guidance of experienced writers. Kevin Higgins, Susan Millar DuMars and I have worked on this project from the start but other writers have also come on board at different points along the way and given their support, for example, Jim Mullarkey who facilitated the *Uisce* story. Participative arts is a practice founded above all on collaboration and commitment between various community partners and artists, from planning to process. We are indebted to many people who helped bring this project to completion. We are grateful to The Arts Council of Ireland, who awarded an Arts Participation Bursary to Mary Madec and Aideen Barry; James Harrold, Galway City Arts Officer, Marilyn Gaughan, Galway County Arts Officer and Donal Walshe, Galway VEC Community Education for their encouragement and unstinting support. We are grateful to Ballybane library for hosting the workshops week after week as well as occasional readings and to Over the Edge for inviting and supporting some of the writers to read their work at Open Mic events in the city; to the teachers and staff at the Brothers of Charity Services, Sandra Hayden, Marie Dillon, Elva Glynn, Lisa Goaley, Seán Gibbons and Margaret Costello who support participants and writers with enthusiasm and sensitivity.

This collection gathers individual pieces created by sole authors and group pieces where the final version was produced by several participants working together; the final text is in the words of the participants and represents their creative collaboration. *Jessica Casey* is such a piece. The process of producing the work from the facilitator's point of view was rich and rewarding and a deep learning experience; it also provided insights into the transformative and healing personal journeys which the Arts make possible, and which certainly happened here. Overall, for the participants it brought a whole new sense of what is possible when there is true artistic collaboration, an experience which was engaging, exciting and fun. This piece brings us into the funny phantasmagoric world of a young woman on the threshold of the adult world. It gives us insight into the lives of these authors and what they find interesting and amusing about the world around them.

Engaging with primary experience is essential above all to poetry. In the individual poems in particular you will get many insights into how these writers see, feel, taste and hear the world they live in. Their perspectives are often surprising and moving—from simple everyday experiences of eating (for example John Paul Grealish's poem) or living in the cycles of nature (for example, Peggy Kearney's *Ballyturn Summer*) to assumed personae as in Paddy McDonagh's, *My Name is Rose*. Our poetry reflects the deepest things that go on inside us, our most developed feelings, our highest ideals. Sometimes the poets in this volume inhabit their images with stunning confidence and humility as in David Cormican's winning poem, *I am an Ash Tree*. Poetry also develops an ability to observe and listen to others as well as to oneself. It teaches empathy and compassion when we engage with it as a collaborative participative practice. Reading the work of others is a kind of listening and initiates a dialogue between us and other writers; our work speaks out of, and into this space, and this dynamic situates us in a tradition. There are some poems in this volume which are responses to the work of others, such as Mary Kinsella's poem, *The Wind of Coole* or Bernard Deering's poem *Man*.

Last December three of our writers came in First, Second and shared Third in the Inclusion Ireland Poetry Awards—David Cormican took First for his poem, *I am an Ash Tree* but sadly passed away before he got the good news, Sharon Murray took Second for her poem, *Sad* and Bernard Deering, the Third Prize for his poem, *Man*. There were also other poems which made the short list. They are included in this collection. But in our book—this book—all the writers are winners and their inclusion here is a celebration of what it means for them to participate in a practice which is so esteemed and so culturally embedded in our society, a practice which expresses in their own words their journey as human beings in the world.

Finally I like to think of this anthology and DVD as a way to share the experiences of the writers and facilitators of the Jessica Casey project and of the poetry workshops. Besides the educational and cultural benefits, there were personal and spiritual benefits for all the participants who engaged in the process. When taken seriously, writing changes us as people, as creators who listen to the rumblings of our own hearts and as readers who listen to others. This is true for everyone without exception. So I would like to think of this volume also as a democratic gesture, validating the lives and experiences of these contributors and the journeys they have made to produce this work. I hope it gives them their rightful place in the world of writing.

MARY MADEC

Jessica Casey... An animated life

The project *Jessica Casey* was one that intrigued me from the outset. How the writers from the AWAY WITH WORDS project created such a detailed and yet exaggerated character, that seemed so true to many modern characterisations of the ditzy materialistic super femme fatale, seemed amazing to me. This creature was one of wonder, and her creators had defined her right down to the additional few inches of her manicured nails.

Jessica Casey is a *tour de force*, not someone to be ignored, and certainly not someone you would go to for fashion advice. She embodies the pure humour and wit of the writers who moulded her from their fertile imaginations.

The writing of *Jessica Casey* made the transition from two dimensional text to three dimensional action quite an easy one. We had looked at some of the films of Buster Keaton and Charlie Chaplin for inspiration when considering how *Jessica Casey* should move and interact with her fellow characters. However colour became a very important factor too when considering how to make the animated actions. Of course Jessica herself doesn't do pastel, so we had to make sure that whenever we shot the animated gestures, that the colours were exaggerated in a way that lent itself to Jessica's personality: LOUD, BOLD and often TASTELESS!

AIDEEN BARRY

*"You have to inhabit poetry
if you want to make it."*

ANNE STEVENSON
The Fiction-Makers, 1985

Jessica Casey

by THE DUIRLING WRITERS

Teresa Hopkins
William Devane
Cuimín Flaherty
John Paul Grealish
Oliver Curran
Martin McDonagh
Mícheál Concannon

Meet Jessica Casey

JESSICA CASEY lives in County Mayo, Castlebar in fact. She has a pink hand with long purple nails. She has a dog called Rosie. She turned pink when she touched her with her pink hands. I am a bit worried. I like Jessica Casey. If she touches me what colour will I go? I don't think it will be pink, it will be red.

Jessica's Secrets

Jessica Casey has a lot of secrets. First of all she's an underage driver. "It's against the law," says Martin. "She shouldn't be on the road, "says Teresa. "I was going to report her to the guards," says Michael, "when she took off." She put on her pink lipstick and she gave an evil smile. William says, "Let's give her another chance, she's such a babe!" "I agree," says John-Paul, "and I want to marry her." "I'll be the first one to marry her," says William. "If I was a guard, I'd chase her and give her the kiss of life," says Michael. "Cop on to yourselves," says Cumín, "she's crazy as Kate Perry." "Keep after her," says Oliver, "and may the best man get her." Jessica has one other BIG secret. She has a smoking habit. TWENTY cigarettes a day. First thing in the morning she creeps out the door before anyone is up and smokes three in a row. "Now, I'm ready for the day," she thinks as she rushes back in to have a shower (good for getting rid of the smell!)

Jessica longs for an iPhone

Jessica Casey loves to text. However she is finding it hard to do with her long purple nails. "I need to get an iPhone," she says. Secretly, 'a smart phone for a smart girl,' she thinks. She's tired of the shortcuts. Instead of **cul8r** she could write easily with her touch screen and predictive text, *See you later alligator!* She heads off to the CarPhone Warehouse all excited. The assistant explains the two options, bill pay or pay as you go. On Bill pay it will cost her 99 euro and on 65 euro a month. On Pay As You Go it will cost her 500 euro. She's horrified. "Where will I get the money?" she thinks secretly. "I'll have a think about it," she says to the assistant. She leaves the shop with her heart in her UGG boots.

Jessica plans a holiday

Jessica Casey is planning a holiday. She's flicking through the brochures. The Algarve looks good. Barcelona sounds, 'awesome.' Jessica likes the word 'awesome.' Ibiza looks like a good place – *the island that never sleeps*. Secretly she thinks about the bikini she'll get and that lovely sundress she saw on the Littlewoods site. And what about sunglasses? She saw a pair in Boots, Armani with huge round frames – 'awesome', perfect for looking at the cool dudes over in Ibiza. She imagines herself sipping cocktails by the pool. Piña Colada would taste perfect. Of course she'll need a suntan before she goes. "I can't wait to get there," she thinks. Then she remembers that the credit card is maxed out, her bank account is overdrawn. Maybe she'll have to clip those purple nails and get down to work. "Whoa. This isn't good at all," she thinks.

Jessica, a farmerette – never!

Jessica Casey clips her purple nails. She checks the *Farmer's Journal* – she loves cows – and finds a vacancy for a farm hand. She decides to call the farmer – he's called Dan." Hello Dan, I'm enquiring about the job in the *Farmer's Journal.*" Dan is surprised and shocked. "Are you sure you have the right number," he says. "Course I have. You are Dan, aren't you?" "Yes....You'd be doing a lot of hard work. Have you ever fed animals, cleaned the byre, put slurry on the fields?" "Ahm, no," she says, realizing that farming is not for her. She's horrified at the thought of the slurry. "Maybe I'll have a think about it," she says. "Do that girl," Dan says laughing. He knows he won't hear from her again. She puts down the phone and says, "No way, José". Maybe she'll try for Supermacs after all.

Jessica wants to reinvent herself

Jessica is SOO excited. She's going for a makeover with Xposé. Not that she needs a makeover she thinks looking at her purple nails... X is waiting for her. "We'll have to do something about these purple nails," she says. Two inches is too long. They're like claws." Jessica openly protests. "It took me two years to grow these," she whimpers. "Need to change that hairstyle too," says X. "Maybe we could give you a fringe?" Jessica is dismayed. X brings her to the mirror. "I think you'd look better in a slightly bigger size." "That's it, I'm out of here," says Jessica as she storms out stomping her feet, flicking her bangs and waving goodbye to X with her long purple nails.

Jessica dreams of better things

Jessica heads off for an early night with a big mug of hot chocolate. She's asleep in a jiffy. Oh boy (or oh girl) she has sweet dreams.

She has won the lotto. Is it 4 million? She was asleep but she was jumping for joy, kicking the covers off. She could see the money sign, $$$$$$$$$$

She can see a CAR… *fuck you Honda Civic, I've a Bugatti Veron outside.* She's head-banging to the *Rubber Bandits*. She can see a house, well a palace and she is the Queen of the *Rubber Bandits*. She's talking in her dreams and she's telling the king, *to get his hole out of my house* like in the *Republic of Telly*.

She can see an elephant with a parasol to cover her head from the sun. This is her dream holiday but it's hot, very hot.

She wakes up and she is sweating. Soaked. Worse still, she realizes that it was all a dream. No lotto. No money. She starts crying, Oh boy (or girl), back to reality…..

Jessica's invitation to the Duirling Hallowe'en Party

Jessica got an invitation on her FB wall to the Duirling Hallowe'en Party. She feels sick about it. Sick but excited. She can't wait. She wants to impress the lads, all six of them. What costume will she wear? She could be a witch but she might scare the six lads. She could be a pumpkin but they'd cut her up with a knife. She could be a ghost but then she'd be anonymous. They wouldn't see her legs. She'd be as wide as a bus. "O Happy Days, I have it. I'll be a cat-woman" she says, "all black with a mask. Black gloves up to my biceps. White high heels. With platforms. Black satin leggings. PURR-fect! I'll be a Babe."

Jessica is going to the Maam Cross Fair

Jessica is going to the Maam Cross Fair. She wants to see what the big fuss is about. She dresses up, sits into her Honda, turns on the ignition and revs up the engine. She speeds down the road to Leenane, screeches to a halt and turns left for Maam. She's going up and down the hills like a roller-coaster. She feels *mountain-sick* but gets excited when she sees the stalls and the animals in the distance. "Oh My God, I'm here at last," she says. She's starving so she heads straight for Cumín's chipper. "Fabulous chips," she says, gobbling them in big mouthfuls. She sees a jewellery stall, chains, earrings, bracelets, rings. "Cheap," she thinks to herself. She goes to the perfume stall. All watered-down. She's not impressed. She spots a car stall and she sees a spoiler and tinted windows that she likes. She asks what price they are but she doesn't have the money. She's disappointed. She hops back into her car and takes off as fast as she came. "The only good thing about the day was the chips at Cumín's chipper," she thinks. "Don't think I'll be going back there next year," she says, banging the door shut.

Invitation to Aussieland

Jessica hears a letter coming through the door. "Oh My God, I wonder what's in the letter..?" She opens it up but she doesn't recognize the hand-writing. She rips it open with her long purple nails. It reads:

Dear Jessica,
Howdy mate? Sit down before you read THIS. Remember me? I'm Cindy from Sydney and we met at the Tea Gardens Pub. Guess what? I won the lotto and I want you to come visit me. ALL on me! Honest to God. So pull your finger out and get down to USIT. I can't wait to see you mate. First night a barbie on Bondi Beach. Second night we'll meet the cast of Home and Away *on Summer Bay.*
Hugo is tall and hot. And your friend William might get to meet Angelo!
Get up now and get with the programme. I'm waiting for you mate. Let's get this party started. I'll ring you about the money stuff.
Love you long time,
Cindy

Dear Cindy,
I'm off to Sydney. Can't wait to see you. You're a fantastic friend. You're so generous. I'm packing my bags already! I know exactly what I'll wear for Bondi Beach (I'll bring my sarong so I make a good impression – know what I mean. Would you like me to take anything over? Barry's teabags? Rashers? Custard Creams? I'm off to USIT now to book my trip. Can't wait... I'm going to land down under very soon.
Lots of love,
Jessica

Jessica is going to find herself

Jessica Casey has a cool idea. A GREAT idea. She licks her fingers and everything changes to pink...and she clicks her fingers again and she lands in the castle of the Dragon's Den. She produces her own brand of lipstick, *LIP LUSH* which changes colour with mood. If you like someone your lips turn pink but if you love them your lips turn red. If you don't like them they'll turn blue. She'd have an insert to explain, *Read My Lips*.......

Jessica wants to change her life

Jessica's tired of flicking her bangs and clicking her nails. She's tired of not achieving things. She wants something more. She wants to make a difference in the world. She wants to spend her life to pray for peace. She needs a break. Inspiration. Praise the Lord, Hallelujah! She's going to join the Poor Clares... Has she got a vocation? Has she the will-power? Would she miss going out on the town clubbing? She wouldn't be able to wear makeup or lipstick or nail varnish or jewellery. And she wouldn't be able to show off her hair....

These are two pathways of life for Jessica. Which one will she decide on?

What do you think she will choose?

Group Poems

Recipe for Morning

If you're groggy and grumpy
And dreading the day
Splash cold water on your face
To wake yourself up,
Put on *Galway Girl*
And dance a jig
Around the kitchen
Then you'll feel on top
Of the world
Ready for whatever treat
The day has in store.

A Frosty Morning

The mist of the hills
Rising from the burren

A soft pile of white carpet
Growing on the car

A Grey squirrel
gathers nuts, freezing in the cold

Hallowe'en Night

Leaf
Yellow brown
Soft rotten sound
Dancing through the air
In circles

Spooky
Doors banging
Is it wind?
I see shadows too
Run

His button is navy
It fell off a coat
I sewed it on a cardigan
It fell off the cardigan
I sewed it on the jacket
It fell off the jacket
I sewed it back again
It stayed on then

Apples on strings
Green, yellow, red
Want a bite?
Jump!

Winter

The birds are quiet
The grass stops growing
The evenings get darker
The nights longer
Leaves change colour and fall
Wind howls through the chimney
And whistles through the door
I shiver and shake off the rain
Have a hot whiskey
With cloves and hot lemon
Wrap myself in a duvet
And hibernate
See you in the Spring

Ten Things to do in Eyre Square

Shop in the food shops
Walk through from the fountain
on Saturdays with Dad
Catch the number three bus
to Ballybrit
Go out for lunch on your own
Just sit down and relax your mind
In the warm weather, lie in the grass
and look up at the sky
Go see the Saw Doctors!
Give out that there's no parking
Feed the pigeons
Watch them fly away

Uisce

This is a story about a man named JOHNNY.
He doesn't have much hair.
He lives in a red house.
He sleeps downstairs with his hands under his head.
What does he normally eat?
He eats fish and chips on a Friday.

He lives with his Ma.
His Ma is nice.
She says, 'Listen here.' Why does she say that to him?
'Why did you come home late?'
Why does he come home late?
Why did he come home late? He got told off. God only
knows that.

His house across the bridge. What church is that?
In a row of houses.
When he looks out his window he sees birdies *agus uisce*,
The river flowing free.
See the water. Gawan—
Swans,
Galway cathedral above the rooftops.

He's getting the bus. He races for it. *Hurry up. Hurry up.*
The Carraroe bus. *Don't be late.*
Otherwise the bus will go without you.
He sees a lot of boats on the way.
That's the reflection. That's beautiful.
You wouldn't be going swimming in that water.

A wet day. It was raining. There's a puddle there.
You don't want to get your shoes wet. No.
The sun came out in Barna.
That's the beach there now.

He sees a boat on its side, a seaweed, a rope.
That's the wall. He can hardly keep his eyes open. Breezy
out there. A cloud.
That's where rain comes from. What holds the stones together?

He remembers Rosmuc. That's where Johnny's mother is from.
Trees and the smooth water and mountains. On a good day.
But today was a bit mucky.

Johnny got off the bus to go for a walk. Up a path. Oh boyo.
The fence holds the stones together.
He met a lovely donkey.
Two lovely donkeys.
Sorry I have no apples for you.

He goes up a hill
Up
And up
You wouldn't want to fall down into that water.
Help.

You'd be swept away. Lord have mercy on him.
Would you like to fall in there? No way. You'd hurt your leg –
Help. Let me out of here. Quick. You might as well. Aah
no! Aah no, is right!
I'm never going to that place again. That'll be the day.
Down he goes sideways. And on and on.

And out into the sea.
The blue
Blue sea
Out where the fish live. All different colours. And
shapes.
And the big fish
That loves the sunrise
And the sunset
That brought Johnny
Back to Galway.

He was very wet and cold. He was shivering.
His mother said, 'Wash yourself,
Change your clothes now.'
Johnny was still showering.
'You'll get cold, you will,' she said.

Johnny was coughing. 'Agh, agh.' His mother said, 'Are
you still right?'
'Weagh a a,' said Johnny.
'You'll not be feeling well.'
'There'll be something wrong with you.' That's what
his mother said,
'What'll the doctor say?'

'Agh, agh', said Johnny,
'He'll get medicine.'
'You'll have to go to the chemist for that.'
'Agh,' says Johnny.
The doctor said, 'How did you get the cough?'
'Sore throat. Sick,' said Johnny.
'Shivering in the water.'
'Agh,' said the doctor.

Johnny got hot medicine. It was nice. He boiled the
kettle. Hot medicine.

Limericks from Galway

There was a young fella from Carna
Who decided he'd move on to Barna
The reason is clear he liked to be near
A beautiful girl called Lorna

A beautiful girl called Kate
Who married Prince William of late
Arrived in her carriage
In time for her marriage
She was never late for a date

For Michael

Michael you're an adult now
You need to act your age
You're twenty-one so take a bow
and walk out on the stage.

I know that you have lots of plans
You'll have to get an age-card
And swimming lessons to teach the fans
And show them you're a life-guard

The girls will screech with sheer delight
When they're drowning in the pool
You'll give them the kiss of life
They'll say, 'That guy is cool.'

Poems for Others

"And did you get
what you wanted from this life, even so?
I did.
And what did you want?
To call myself beloved, to feel myself
Beloved on the earth."

RAYMOND CARVER
'Late fragment'

For Julie

I wish you flowers in the Spring,
Summer sunshine,
Yellow and red autumn leaves,
And an open fire in the winter

I wish you happiness always.

OLIVER CURRAN

For Kathleen

Let's talk business
About Kathleen.
Help her
To calm down.

MARTIN MCDONAGH

For Róisín

You are funny
And caring
And I love when you say, 'Hee, haw!'
To make me laugh
When you take my photo.

For Claudia

I like to ride the motorbike
With you Claudia
Swerving on the turns
On the windy road in Rosmuc
Going like the hammers
Until we come to a sudden
Halt.

TERESA HOPKINS

Gone

I like oranges juicy and sweet
And flowers in the garden
And the woolly coat of my dog
Who's gone now
My Dad had him.
My Dad's gone
And my mother.
All gone.

Paddy

In Winter I remember you with Mam
In Spring I remember you travelling on the bus
In Summer I remember you on the farm
In Autumn I remember you smoking the pipe
I remember your face was nice and friendly
I remember your smell was clean.
Missing you is like blueness and unhappy
Remembering you is like family events, happy.

Johnny

In winter I remember you helping out on the farm
In Spring I remember you coming home
For a holiday
In Summer you were busy making the hay
In Autumn I remember you at home
I remember your face looked like mine
I remember your voice was full of song
I remember your happy smile.
Missing you is lonely.
When I remember you, I feel sad.

Martin

In Winter I remember you tending the fire
In Spring I remember you did carpentry for Fás
In Summer you took me to London for my birthday
In Autumn you brought me to school
I remember your face looked like mine
I remember your voice, it was soft
I remember your smell, nice aftershave.
Missing you is black
A rainy day.

Single Poems

SECTION 1

Inclusion Ireland Winners

"What is the language using us for?
It uses us all and in its dark
Of dark actions selections differ.

I am not making a fool of myself
For you. What I am making is
A place for language in my life."

W.S GRAHAM
'What is the Language Using us for?'

DAVID CORMICAN

I am an Ash Tree

I am a tall ash tree full of leaves
I am in a forest
It is dark and brown
My roots are forming
My trunk is my work
My bark is gentle and kind
My branches are creative writing, meeting friends and traditional music.
My leaves are sadness and shyness.
It is winter and I stand in the cold, alone but happy.

Second Prize

SHARON MURRAY

Sad

I am sad because my little cousin Lauren
is in hospital.

And the black crows have taken all the food
from the little robins.

BERNARD DEERING

Man

after William Blake

Cruelty has a cat's heart
that plays with rats.
Jealousy is a woman.
Strong, posh and dangerous.
Terror is a cat's crawl.
Claws, eyes on my shoulder.
Secrecy is an old man
guarding his own business.
Man is broken in two.
He is happy and sad.
His human face is a burning sun,
but the human heart is broken.

SECTION 2

People Who Inspire

"I listen to whatever makes you talk—
whatever that is—and me listen"

SHINKICHI TAKAHASHI
'Words'

Mystery Man

Hey scuba diver!
I like you because
You're my friend.

Remember when you took me back the shell
That I keep in my bedroom.
I think about you and wonder
Will I meet you again
Down by the seashore

You look so good in your wetsuit.
You can move so quickly,
Splashing under the water.
And see all the colours
Beneath the sea.

The man she could not remember

Sandra went to bed feeling very tired. She fell asleep and started to dream. Night was falling and she could not find her way out of the deep forest. As Sandra went deeper into the dream, she went deeper into the forest until she came to a castle on top of a hill.

Sandra went up to the door, knocked on the door and the door slowly opened. Sandra walked inside. Then she heard a voice saying, "Come in."

Sandra looked around but she could see no-one. Then this man with a black robe with a hat always on his head appeared from nowhere. Sandra heard the door close behind her. She got a fright. Then the voice said again, "Do not be afraid, I will not hurt you."

Sandra turned around and there was the most beautiful man she had ever seen in her whole life, standing behind her with a hood on his head. "Do not be frightened," the man said and he took the hood off his head, there in front of her. The most beautiful man that Sandra had ever seen took her hand and then went dancing with her. But he let her hand go, Sandra woke from her dream and was in bed.

The next morning Sandra was shopping and she saw the same man walking up the street but she could not remember where she had seen him before.

PADDY MCDONAGH

My name is Rose

My hair is black.
I talk fast.
When I talk I say, 'Thanks for the memories.'

I am five foot six tall
and cross-eyed.
I like to drink tea.
I like to eat bacon and cabbage.
I wear yellow every day.
I am paid to type.
I wear old comfy shoes, left and right foot.

I go to the pub twice a week
and my favourite drink is whiskey.
I have to take a taxi home,
to row home in a shoe.

I have no boyfriend
but I have a crooked cat
and a tobacco pipe.

Brown Cloaks and Carry Hats

You paid twelve pounds for the hats they wear.
They thank you for the cloaks you gave them.
They come to the door and you give them sweets.

The cloaks they wear.
You give them a hive hat.
They give you two hats.

The cloaks we don't wear,
we leave them on the heater
to be hung up.

ANNE MARIE JORDAN

You are my sunshine

It makes you happy
To sing it out loud.
It makes you glow,

Because sun makes you smile
like a hummingbird
And it feels so great to sing,

You are my sunshine, my only sunshine.

Eamon O'Sullivan

The Secret

My name is Pete
I am mad
I am locked up
I like to look out the window
I am a bad man
I hate someone
I don't have a bed
I sleep on a long cushion
I am sad because I am locked up for the rest of my time
The secret I have is murder.

What I find difficult

The deaths of my people.
My grandmother died.
Cruelty.
Somebody had left the country.
Violence.
We said goodbye to Josie Doherty,
Tears coming out of our eyes.
The baby was crying because his sister had died.
When the series ends with sadness, for the Summer, until
the Autumn.
When we leave we go away for a while.

Summer

I went to the Galway Races with Noelle
by helicopter
and I had the winning bet.

Noelle and I.
It was nice. I enjoyed it.
It was very hot and I sweated a lot.

What will help me remember?
A helicopter. Any helicopter.

Locket

The Blessed Virgin
Heart-shape
On a chain
Silver
An angel with a cross
Put a picture of The Lady in it.
Light a candle.
My sister and my brother are in my heart.
Eleanor and Dick are dead and gone.
I say a prayer for them.

Section 3

Ordinary Life

"And here is love,
like a tinsmith's scoop
sunk past its gleam
in the meal-bin"

Seamus Heaney
'Mossbawn'

Dream Kitchen

I'd like a new kitchen, please.
Red. All red. Countertop and all.
Blue tiles under the cabinets
And cream tiles on the floor.
I'd like to order the cupboards
And have a bin system.

I'd like a very big fridge
That can make cold drinks
I'd keep the wine and lager in there.
Ooh la la!

Orange

I am the sun
I am round in the centre
I look like an orange
I feel sharp
I see churches and hills
I hear birds singing
My job is to make things grow
At night I go down between the clouds
When it is cloudy you cannot see me
My favourite thing to do is to give a tan
If I could say, 'I shine in your eyes.'

Mmmm...

I like the smell of pancakes,
And cheese on toast
And even tuna.
Now I'm hungry
Let's eat something
Anything

OLIVER CURRAN

Fruit Bowl

I like pear-shaped
And apple-shaped
And the shape of banana
And the little ovals of grapes
All in a curved bowl.

RONAN SCANNELL

Blue Paint

I feel sad when people talk rubbish.
When I feel sad, I give out.
Cars make me feel better.
Sad is blue.
It feels lonely.
It sounds like shouting.
It tastes like blue paint.

SECTION 4

Nature around us

"The Bud Stands for all things"

GALWAY KINNELL

Mary Kinsella

The Wind of Coole

Oh Lady of Coole
Blowing in the wind,
How I see you
In everything there is.

In the Seven Woods
You still walk there,
The wind still blows you
Through my hair.

Oh be still wind of Coole
Shine your smile on the water,
As the lady stands
To watch the swans
Swimming in the lonely pool.

As night falls
They fly away,
The lady of the wind says,
Come back and stay.

Ballyturn Summer

Lively days playing with Shane,
walking with Lassie,
helping Maura get the dinner,
hoovering the rooms.

My home overlooking the lake
with waterlilies,
peace and tranquillity there.
Summer rain falls on the lake
bursts into sunshine.

Having a Sky Day

i.
The sun and moon inhabit
The four provinces of the world.
The West is warm
The North a bit colder
East is just about
South a warm breeze

ii.
Half moon is harvest time,
then a full moon before it wanes.
There's a face on the moon.
The sun is yellow, it keeps us warm.

iii.
Father and Mother under the rainbow.
They like the colours of the rainbow.
Father and Mother together match the rainbow.
Colour covers them:
violet
orange
indigo
yellow
maroon

EDMUND HENRY

The Sun

My heart jumps a beat
When I see the sunshine
Yellow and bright

When I was small
I ran outside
To see the sun

I used to imagine
What it was like
To touch

But now I am a grown man
I know
It can burn

My heart jumps
A beat
When I see the sun

Meditation On Birds Of Flight

Pigeons and doves belong to the same family.
White doves are released on occasions of ceremony.

We have small blackberries on a tree at the back of our house.
They attract pigeons and the collared dove.

Swallows line up on the clothesline
then swoop and climb the air.

The stork flies low, stands on one leg.
I like to go out and about.

CORA LALLY

Postcard

Palau in Sardegna,
Seaside like Galway
With the Aran islands in the distance.

Pink roses on the right-hand corner of the card,
Seawater between the land and the islands,

A spread of houses on the coast.

ANNE-MARIE JORDAN

Autumn

I hear the leaves
Shuffling as they scatter
We walk and trample on them
On the ground beneath us
What a lovely sight to see
All the colours,
Brown, green, wine.
We touch them, sometimes velvet
Sometimes rough like sandpaper,
Then let them fall quietly to the ground.

WILLIAM DEVANE

Sensational

I like waxy soft leaves
And rough bark
And the short silky coat
Of our Connemara pony
The leather seats on the bus
As I sit in
To come here to the Duirling.

SECTION 5

Pets

Messe agus Pangur Bán,
cechtar nathar fria shaindán:
bíth a menmasam fri seilgg,
mu menma céin im shaincheirdd.

I and Pangur Bán, my cat
'Tis a like task we are at;
Hunting mice is his delight
Hunting words I sit all night

WRITTEN BY AN UNKNOWN IRISH MONK, A STUDENT OF THE MONASTERY
OF CARINTHIA, ON A COPY OF ST PAUL'S EPISTLES CIRCA 9TH CENTURY.
Translation Robin Flower.

I am a man with nine cats

They have eighty-one lives
John and Edward (they look the same),
Cascarino, Smokey, Bluebell, Patches,
Felix, Bunty and Twista.
Cascarino eats inside—she's a bit of a snob
She hits the others with her paw and growls
(in as far as a cat growls)
But she loves us.
She comes up on my lap
And tries to kiss me.
I say, "No, thank you!
I like you but not that much!"

OLIVER CURRAN

Mo mhaidirín Coco

Tagann sé go dtí an geata
Agus mar go bhfuil se beag
Léimeann sé ar an bpiléar
Chun failtiú romham
Ag tafann agus ag croidheadh a eireball,
Gaisce mór aige.

My Little Dog Coco

Comes to the gate
And as he's small
He jumps up on the pillar to wait
Barks with excitement
Wags his tail.
Proud and delighted
to see me.

If

If you see a magpie at night
the cat catches mice

If you see robin redbreast during the day
you'd talk to him

He'd open his beak and speak
'Don't worry about it,' he'd say.

HILARY MURRAY

This Summer

This summer I will go horse-riding
down to the stables,
saddle on pony,
cane in hand.
Off we trot.
Over the fences,
down to Tracht Beach.

CHARLIE COOLEY

Untitled 02/06/09

An angel hugging the moon
high in the sky.
It is not night-time not
yellow like
the butter and the sun.
There is a church
the picture makes me thrilled
the town

SECTION 6

A Journey, A Pilgrimage

"Pilgrim remember
For all your pain
The Master you seek abroad
You will find at home—
Or walk in vain"

ANONYMOUS, 7th Century

ANGELA WILSON

Miracle of Rome

I always wanted to go to Rome but I didn't know what to expect. I was worried at the same time that I wouldn't be able to manage because I had a sore leg but I said, "Yes, yes, yes!"

The first thing that struck me when we arrived at our little hotel was the lovely hospitality. Georgia, who was from Romania, was so charming and had a big smile for us. She showed us where we were sleeping and brought us down to a restaurant. We sampled all the Italian food. My favourite dish was ice cream!

The first day we went to St. Peter's Square and I was fascinated. We went inside and saw Pope John XXIII laid out in a glass tomb. Also we saw the Pièta – it was white and lovely. Eugene said that Michelangelo was like me with the curly hair! Eugene was in Rome last year.

I enjoyed taking photographs but sometimes it was very hard because there were so many people going past and I was afraid I'd lose everyone else.

We visited the Vatican Museum and we had our own tour guide. She was tall and it was easy to see her. The thing I remember most is what she told us about Michelangelo. We saw the Sistine Chapel and the Vatican Gardens. We saw maps of Italy in the Museum. We saw lots of beautiful marble statues with nothing on them but a smile, sometimes not even a smile! We went to see the

Pantheon with its hole in the ceiling. It was two thousand years old – amazing!

At the Trevi Fountain I threw in a coin over my left shoulder so that I'd see Rome again. While I was there an Italian photographer came and took my photo and you can see the horse statues in the background. On the card that he gave me with my photo there is also a picture of Pope John Paul II and Pope Benedict XVI.

The Coliseum wasn't my favourite place when I heard that they once killed the Christians there. I felt nervous going up the lifts and looking down through the big windows. A scary place!

It was so warm that we had lunch out every day. One day we had sandwiches in front of the French Cultural Centre and another day on the steps of a church near St. Peter's Square.

On the Sunday we went to the canonization mass of five people in St. Peter's Square. It was so packed we didn't even get communion! It was hard to see anything and it was very hot. I had to leave for a drink.

The day before we left Georgia got a local woman to cook us up an Italian meal. In the evening before bed we chatted to Georgia and Giuseppe. In fact Giuseppe made my cappuccino for me every morning!

It was a pure miracle how the pain left my leg before I travelled to Rome. In the end I was even able to manage without the walking stick. When I came home everyone said it was the miracle of Rome!

RAYMOND ALLEN is from Leitirmore but spent many years up the country! He loves music, drama, art and writing.

AIFRIC HENRY BRUEN is currently in Transition Year in Coláiste Iognáid, Galway. She enjoys running and rowing at school. She is interested in acting and recently joined Galway Youth Theatre. She played Cindy in the animation and was wardrobe consultant throughout.

PÁDRAIG CLARKE is from Mackney, Ballinasloe. He likes computers, music and people. His favourite hobby is socializing!

MÍCHEÁL CONCANNON is from Furbo. He loves soccer (he's a Liverpool fan) and Honda Civic cars! He likes boxing, dancing and going out to dinner. He loves all kinds of dance music and Mick Flavin (when he's not dancing).

CHARLIE COOLEY is from Galway. He enjoys the outdoors and walking and putting order on things.

DAVID CORMICAN was from Clarinbridge and attached to Clarenmore Centre. He grew up on a farm and always had a love of nature. He had the true heart of a poet. He died in October 2011.

OLIVER CURRAN is from Spiddal. He loves jigsaws, the harder the better. He also loves music and his favourite song is 'Summertime'. He's always up for a joke and you'll make him very happy if you give him chocolate cake.

BERNARD DEERING comes from Wicklow but has lived in Galway for many years. He loves painting and writing and is a big fan of red wine.

WILLIAM DEVANE is the youngest of a family of 14 and lives on a lively farm in Carna. He's a 'soapaholic' and follows all the details of these exciting screen lives. He loves people and can be persuaded to do some sean nós dancing.

PAUL DUNNE is from Headford and loves technology. He enjoys taking videos and setting up sound for music events.

CUIMÍN FLAHERTY comes from Camus. He's a hard worker and an expert on recycling. He loves walking but also spinning in the bus. Above all he is an artist who loves his art passionately. When he's not too busy he loves to work with his Dad selling fish and chips.

JOHN FLANNERY comes form Headford, plays soccer and is a dedicated Manchester United fan. He loves working in the library.

JOHN PAUL GREALISH is from Rosmuc and he has a twin sister. He loves drama, hoovering (a good man around the house!), bowling and cinema.

FRANCES GREENE is from Moore Co. Roscommon. She likes flowers, gardening, art and, of course, writing.

JOE GREENE is from Carraroe and has returned to live there recently to be near his family. He loves singing and writing.

EDMUND HENRY comes from Galway city. He finds history and geography very interesting and loves travelling.

TERESA HOPKINS was born in England and came back in the mid-nineties to Connemara. She loves handbags and getting her hair done, and... an odd glass of wine.

ANNE-MARIE JORDAN comes from New Quay in the Burren. She loves clothes, jewellery, nature and writing and... Jedward!

GERALD JOYCE was born in London and half his heart is still over there! He loves Madonna and Cilla Black!

PEGGY KEARNEY is from Ballyturn, Co. Clare. She loves dogs and jewellery.

PADDY KELLY comes from Ballinasloe but lives in Athenry and has been interested in writing for a long time. He published a collection of his poetry called Paddy's Poems in December 2011 available anytime from the author!

MARY KINSELLA lives in Gort and has been writing for as long as she can remember. Her dream is to write a play for performance.

CORA LALLY is from Whitestrand Avenue, Salthill. She likes knitting, sewing and baking lots of goodies.

SÍOFRA LEONARD is also in Transition Year in Coláiste Iognáid, Galway. She lives a life full of activity – Gaelic football, basketball, hockey, camogie. She is always up for trying new things and enjoyed playing Jessica in the animation!

MARTIN MCDONAGH is from Rossaveal and a wonderful Country and Western singer. He once went to Nashville, Tennessee. He loves tandem cycling and went to France with a group from NCBI last year.

PADDY MCDONAGH is from the Claddagh in Galway. He loves participating in Macnas events and playing the Barrel Organ. He has been serving Mass at Galway Cathedral for many years.

BILLY MCGAGH was born in New York. He is a Liverpool fan and likes walking and basketball.

JIMMY MOHAN comes from Mayo and loves gardening and the outdoors.

ANNIE MULREENAN comes from Castlerea, likes shopping for clothes and lighting candles in the church.

HILARY MURRAY loves to chat. She comes from Kinvara and is a big Daniel O'Donnell fan.

SHARON MURRAY is from Peterswell, Co. Galway. She loves her laptop and enjoys games and word-searches!

EAMONN O'SULLIVAN is from Kerry, loves music and plays the accordion.

RONAN SCANNELL is from Galway city, has discerning taste in cars and loves holidays in France.

ANGELA WILSON is from Tuam and has lived in Galway for many years. She has a wonderful cat called Lucky and enjoys a good waltz. She has been writing for many years and still enjoys the workshop.

AIDEEN BARRY is a Visual Artist based in the west of Ireland. Aideen is known nationally and internationally for her practise as a contemporary artist. Her work has won numerous awards including the COE Award, the Project New Work Award from the Arts Council of Ireland, the Silent Light Film Award from the Cork Film Centre, Best Experimental Work 2011 from the San Francisco International Animation Festival, and in 2010 she was shortlisted for the prestigious AIB Prize. Aideen is known not only for her practise as a visual artist but also for her role as advocate for the Visual Arts in Ireland. She lectures in GMIT and Limerick School of Art and Design.

MARY MADEC was born and raised in the west of Ireland. She studied at NUI, Galway (B.A., M.A., H.Dip Ed.) and at the University of Pennsylvania from which she received a doctorate in Linguistics in 2002. She has taught courses for NUI, Galway, Villanova, UPenn and Open University and is currently Director of the Villanova Study Abroad Program in Galway. She has published in *Crannóg, West 47, The Cúirt Annual, Poetry Ireland Review, the SHOp, The Sunday Tribune, Southword, The Cork Literary Review, Iota, Nth Position, Natural Bridge, The Recorder, The Stand* (forthcoming), *Orbis* (forthcoming) and *Cyphers* (forthcoming) and *Poetry Ireland Review* (forthcoming). Her work was solicited for *The Foxchase Review* and *Dogs Singing: A Tribute Anthology* (Salmon, 2010). In Spring 2007 she was chosen for the Poetry Ireland Introductions Series and for the WINDOWS Showcase Readings and Anthology. She has read at Over the Edge and was chosen for the Over the Edge Showcase in 2008. In 2008 she also won the Hennessy XO Award for Emerging Poetry. Her first collection, *In Other Words,* was published by Salmon in May 2010. She has read her work widely most recently at the Clifden Arts Festival 2011 and at the American Conference for Irish Studies 2012. With her husband, Claude Madec she started up a community-writing project, *Away with Words*, now in its fifth year.

About the DVD

The Animated Short "Jessica Casey" was created with the collaboration of the AWAY WITH WORDS Collective and visual artist AIDEEN BARRY. Shot over a period of weeks with members of the collective and with two very talented young actors SÍOFRA LEONARD and AIFRIC HENRY BRUEN. This moving image project was created by employing techniques in stop motion animation. The group were very much inspired by the films of Charlie Chaplin and Buster Keaton and it was this influence that dictated how our protagonist 'Jessica Casey' would engage with the world that the Away With Words group had created. The short is loosely based on the accompanying story of Jessica Casey, and tracks her adventures of getting a job on a working farm, her attempts to earn a living, or drive a car and her struggle to get to Australia to go clubbing with her mate Cindy!